GNU Grep

A catalogue record for this book is available from the Hong Kong Public Libraries.

Published in Hong Kong by Samurai Media Limited.

Email: info@samuraimedia.org

ISBN 978-988-8381-46-3

Background Cover Image by https://www.flickr.com/people/webtreatsetc/

Table of Contents

1 Introduction

grep searches input files for lines containing a match to a given pattern list. When it finds a match in a line, it copies the line to standard output (by default), or produces whatever other sort of output you have requested with options.

Though **grep** expects to do the matching on text, it has no limits on input line length other than available memory, and it can match arbitrary characters within a line. If the final byte of an input file is not a newline, **grep** silently supplies one. Since newline is also a separator for the list of patterns, there is no way to match newline characters in a text.

2 Invoking grep

The general synopsis of the grep command line is

        grep *options* *pattern* *input_file_names*

There can be zero or more *options*. *pattern* will only be seen as such (and not as an *input_file_name*) if it wasn't already specified within *options* (by using the '-e *pattern*' or '-f *file*' options). There can be zero or more *input_file_names*.

2.1 Command-line Options

grep comes with a rich set of options: some from POSIX and some being GNU extensions. Long option names are always a GNU extension, even for options that are from POSIX specifications. Options that are specified by POSIX, under their short names, are explicitly marked as such to facilitate POSIX-portable programming. A few option names are provided for compatibility with older or more exotic implementations.

Several additional options control which variant of the grep matching engine is used. See Section 2.4 [grep Programs], page 12.

2.1.1 Generic Program Information

'--help'   Print a usage message briefly summarizing the command-line options and the bug-reporting address, then exit.

'-V'
'--version'
             Print the version number of grep to the standard output stream. This version number should be included in all bug reports.

2.1.2 Matching Control

'-e *pattern*'
'--regexp=*pattern*'
             Use *pattern* as the pattern. This can be used to specify multiple search patterns, or to protect a pattern beginning with a '-'. ('-e' is specified by POSIX.)

'-f *file*'
'--file=*file*'
             Obtain patterns from *file*, one per line. The empty file contains zero patterns, and therefore matches nothing. ('-f' is specified by POSIX.)

'-i'
'-y'
'--ignore-case'
             Ignore case distinctions, so that characters that differ only in case match each other. Although this is straightforward when letters differ in case only via lowercase-uppercase pairs, the behavior is unspecified in other situations. For example, uppercase "S" has an unusual lowercase counterpart "ſ" (Unicode character U+017F, LATIN SMALL LETTER LONG S) in many locales, and it is unspecified whether this unusual character matches "S" or "s" even though

uppercasing it yields "S". Another example: the lowercase German letter "ß" (U+00DF, LATIN SMALL LETTER SHARP S) is normally capitalized as the two-character string "SS" but it does not match "SS", and it might not match the uppercase letter "" (U+1E9E, LATIN CAPITAL LETTER SHARP S) even though lowercasing the latter yields the former.

'`-y`' is an obsolete synonym that is provided for compatibility. ('`-i`' is specified by POSIX.)

'`-v`'
'`--invert-match`'
> Invert the sense of matching, to select non-matching lines. ('`-v`' is specified by POSIX.)

'`-w`'
'`--word-regexp`'
> Select only those lines containing matches that form whole words. The test is that the matching substring must either be at the beginning of the line, or preceded by a non-word constituent character. Similarly, it must be either at the end of the line or followed by a non-word constituent character. Word-constituent characters are letters, digits, and the underscore.

'`-x`'
'`--line-regexp`'
> Select only those matches that exactly match the whole line. ('`-x`' is specified by POSIX.)

2.1.3 General Output Control

'`-c`'
'`--count`' Suppress normal output; instead print a count of matching lines for each input file. With the '`-v`' ('`--invert-match`') option, count non-matching lines. ('`-c`' is specified by POSIX.)

'`--color[=WHEN]`'
'`--colour[=WHEN]`'
> Surround the matched (non-empty) strings, matching lines, context lines, file names, line numbers, byte offsets, and separators (for fields and groups of context lines) with escape sequences to display them in color on the terminal. The colors are defined by the environment variable `GREP_COLORS` and default to '`ms=01;31:mc=01;31:sl=:cx=:fn=35:ln=32:bn=32:se=36`' for bold red matched text, magenta file names, green line numbers, green byte offsets, cyan separators, and default terminal colors otherwise. The deprecated environment variable `GREP_COLOR` is still supported, but its setting does not have priority; it defaults to '`01;31`' (bold red) which only covers the color for matched text. *WHEN* is '`never`', '`always`', or '`auto`'.

'`-L`'
'`--files-without-match`'
> Suppress normal output; instead print the name of each input file from which no output would normally have been printed. The scanning of each file stops on the first match.

'`-l`'
'`--files-with-matches`'
>Suppress normal output; instead print the name of each input file from which output would normally have been printed. The scanning of each file stops on the first match. ('`-l`' is specified by POSIX.)

'`-m num`'
'`--max-count=num`'
>Stop reading a file after *num* matching lines. If the input is standard input from a regular file, and *num* matching lines are output, `grep` ensures that the standard input is positioned just after the last matching line before exiting, regardless of the presence of trailing context lines. This enables a calling process to resume a search. For example, the following shell script makes use of it:
>
>```
>while grep -m 1 PATTERN
>do
>   echo xxxx
>done < FILE
>```
>
>But the following probably will not work because a pipe is not a regular file:
>
>```
># This probably will not work.
>cat FILE |
>while grep -m 1 PATTERN
>do
>   echo xxxx
>done
>```
>
>When `grep` stops after *num* matching lines, it outputs any trailing context lines. Since context does not include matching lines, `grep` will stop when it encounters another matching line. When the '`-c`' or '`--count`' option is also used, `grep` does not output a count greater than *num*. When the '`-v`' or '`--invert-match`' option is also used, `grep` stops after outputting *num* non-matching lines.

'`-o`'
'`--only-matching`'
>Print only the matched (non-empty) parts of matching lines, with each such part on a separate output line.

'`-c`'
'`--quiet`'
'`--silent`'
>Quiet; do not write anything to standard output. Exit immediately with zero status if any match is found, even if an error was detected. Also see the '`-s`' or '`--no-messages`' option. ('`-q`' is specified by POSIX.)

'`-s`'
'`--no-messages`'
>Suppress error messages about nonexistent or unreadable files. Portability note: unlike GNU `grep`, 7th Edition Unix `grep` did not conform to POSIX, because it lacked '`-q`' and its '`-s`' option behaved like GNU `grep`'s '`-q`' option.[1] USG-style

---

[1] Of course, 7th Edition Unix predated POSIX by several years!

grep also lacked '-q' but its '-s' option behaved like GNU grep's. Portable shell scripts should avoid both '-q' and '-s' and should redirect standard and error output to '/dev/null' instead. ('-s' is specified by POSIX.)

2.1.4 Output Line Prefix Control

When several prefix fields are to be output, the order is always file name, line number, and byte offset, regardless of the order in which these options were specified.

'-b'
'--byte-offset'

>Print the 0-based byte offset within the input file before each line of output. If '-o' ('--only-matching') is specified, print the offset of the matching part itself. When grep runs on MS-DOS or MS-Windows, the printed byte offsets depend on whether the '-u' ('--unix-byte-offsets') option is used; see below.

'-H'
'--with-filename'

>Print the file name for each match. This is the default when there is more than one file to search.

'-h'
'--no-filename'

>Suppress the prefixing of file names on output. This is the default when there is only one file (or only standard input) to search.

'--label=LABEL'

>Display input actually coming from standard input as input coming from file LABEL. This is especially useful when implementing tools like zgrep; e.g.:

```
gzip -cd foo.gz | grep --label=foo -H something
```

'-n'
'--line-number'

>Prefix each line of output with the 1-based line number within its input file. ('-n' is specified by POSIX.)

'-T'
'--initial-tab'

>Make sure that the first character of actual line content lies on a tab stop, so that the alignment of tabs looks normal. This is useful with options that prefix their output to the actual content: '-H', '-n', and '-b'. In order to improve the probability that lines from a single file will all start at the same column, this also causes the line number and byte offset (if present) to be printed in a minimum-size field width.

'-u'
'--unix-byte-offsets'

>Report Unix-style byte offsets. This option causes grep to report byte offsets as if the file were a Unix-style text file, i.e., the byte offsets ignore carriage returns that were stripped. This will produce results identical to running grep on a Unix machine. This option has no effect unless the '-b' option is also used; it has no effect on platforms other than MS-DOS and MS-Windows.

'-Z'
'--null'   Output a zero byte (the ASCII NUL character) instead of the character that
              normally follows a file name. For example, '`grep -lZ`' outputs a zero byte after
              each file name instead of the usual newline. This option makes the output
              unambiguous, even in the presence of file names containing unusual characters
              like newlines. This option can be used with commands like '`find -print0`',
              '`perl -0`', '`sort -z`', and '`xargs -0`' to process arbitrary file names, even those
              that contain newline characters.

2.1.5 Context Line Control

Regardless of how these options are set, `grep` will never print any given line more than
once. If the '-o' ('--only-matching') option is specified, these options have no effect and
a warning is given upon their use.

'-A *num*'
'--after-context=*num*'
              Print *num* lines of trailing context after matching lines.

'-B *num*'
'--before-context=*num*'
              Print *num* lines of leading context before matching lines.

'-C *num*'
'-*num*'
'--context=*num*'
              Print *num* lines of leading and trailing output context.

'--group-separator=*string*'
              When '-A', '-B' or '-C' are in use, print *string* instead of '--' between groups
              of lines.

'--no-group-separator'
              When '-A', '-B' or '-C' are in use, do not print a separator between groups of
              lines.

   Here are some points about how `grep` chooses the separator to print between prefix fields
and line content:

- Matching lines normally use ':' as a separator between prefix fields and actual line
  content.

- Context (i.e., non-matching) lines use '-' instead.

- When context is not specified, matching lines are simply output one right after another.

- When context is specified, lines that are adjacent in the input form a group and are
  output one right after another, while by default a separator appears between non-
  adjacent groups.

- The default separator is a '--' line; its presence and appearance can be changed with
  the options above.

- Each group may contain several matching lines when they are close enough to each
  other that two adjacent groups connect and can merge into a single contiguous one.

2.1.6 File and Directory Selection

'`-a`'

'`--text`' Process a binary file as if it were text; this is equivalent to the '`--binary-files=text`' option.

'`--binary-files=type`'

If a file's allocation metadata, or if its data read before a line is selected for output, indicate that the file contains binary data, assume that the file is of type *type*. Non-text bytes indicate binary data; these are either data bytes improperly encoded for the current locale, or null bytes when the '`-z`' ('`--null-data`') option is not given (see Section 2.1.7 [Other Options], page 8).

By default, *type* is '`binary`', and `grep` normally outputs either a one-line message saying that a binary file matches, or no message if there is no match. When processing binary data, `grep` may treat non-text bytes as line terminators; for example, the pattern '`.`' (period) might not match a null byte, as the null byte might be treated as a line terminator even without the '`-z`' ('`--null-data`') option.

If *type* is '`without-match`', `grep` assumes that a binary file does not match; this is equivalent to the '`-I`' option.

If *type* is '`text`', `grep` processes a binary file as if it were text; this is equivalent to the '`-a`' option.

Warning: '`--binary-files=text`' might output binary garbage, which can have nasty side effects if the output is a terminal and if the terminal driver interprets some of it as commands.

'`-D action`'

'`--devices=action`'

If an input file is a device, FIFO, or socket, use *action* to process it. If *action* is '`read`', all devices are read just as if they were ordinary files. If *action* is '`skip`', devices, FIFOs, and sockets are silently skipped. By default, devices are read if they are on the command line or if the '`-R`' ('`--dereference-recursive`') option is used, and are skipped if they are encountered recursively and the '`-r`' ('`--recursive`') option is used. This option has no effect on a file that is read via standard input.

'`-d action`'

'`--directories=action`'

If an input file is a directory, use *action* to process it. By default, *action* is '`read`', which means that directories are read just as if they were ordinary files (some operating systems and file systems disallow this, and will cause `grep` to print error messages for every directory or silently skip them). If *action* is '`skip`', directories are silently skipped. If *action* is '`recurse`', `grep` reads all files under each directory, recursively, following command-line symbolic links and skipping other symlinks; this is equivalent to the '`-r`' option.

'`--exclude=glob`'

Skip files whose name matches the pattern *glob*, using wildcard matching. When searching recursively, skip any subfile whose base name matches *glob*;

the base name is the part after the last '/'. A pattern can use '*', '?', and '['...']' as wildcards, and \ to quote a wildcard or backslash character literally.

'`--exclude-from=file`'

Skip files whose name matches any of the patterns read from *file* (using wildcard matching as described under '`--exclude`').

'`--exclude-dir=glob`'

Skip any directory whose name matches the pattern *glob*. When searching recursively, skip any subdirectory whose base name matches *glob*. Ignore any redundant trailing slashes in *glob*.

'`-I`'   Process a binary file as if it did not contain matching data; this is equivalent to the '`--binary-files=without-match`' option.

'`--include=glob`'

Search only files whose name matches *glob*, using wildcard matching as described under '`--exclude`'.

'`-r`'
'`--recursive`'

For each directory operand, read and process all files in that directory, recursively. Follow symbolic links on the command line, but skip symlinks that are encountered recursively. Note that if no file operand is given, grep searches the working directory. This is the same as the '`--directories=recurse`' option.

'`-R`'
'`--dereference-recursive`'

For each directory operand, read and process all files in that directory, recursively, following all symbolic links.

2.1.7 Other Options

'`--line-buffered`'

Use line buffering on output. This can cause a performance penalty.

'`-U`'
'`--binary`'

Treat the file(s) as binary. By default, under MS-DOS and MS-Windows, **grep** guesses whether a file is text or binary as described for the '`--binary-files`' option. If grep decides the file is a text file, it strips carriage returns from the original file contents (to make regular expressions with ^ and $ work correctly). Specifying '`-U`' overrules this guesswork, causing all files to be read and passed to the matching mechanism verbatim; if the file is a text file with CR/LF pairs at the end of each line, this will cause some regular expressions to fail. This option has no effect on platforms other than MS-DOS and MS-Windows.

'`-z`'
'`--null-data`'

Treat the input as a set of lines, each terminated by a zero byte (the ASCII NUL character) instead of a newline. Like the '`-Z`' or '`--null`' option, this option can be used with commands like '`sort -z`' to process arbitrary file names.

2.2 Environment Variables

The behavior of grep is affected by the following environment variables.

The locale for category LC_*foo* is specified by examining the three environment variables LC_ALL, LC_*foo*, and LANG, in that order. The first of these variables that is set specifies the locale. For example, if LC_ALL is not set, but LC_COLLATE is set to 'pt_BR', then the Brazilian Portuguese locale is used for the LC_COLLATE category. As a special case for LC_MESSAGES only, the environment variable LANGUAGE can contain a colon-separated list of languages that overrides the three environment variables that ordinarily specify the LC_MESSAGES category. The 'C' locale is used if none of these environment variables are set, if the locale catalog is not installed, or if grep was not compiled with national language support (NLS).

Many of the environment variables in the following list let you control highlighting using Select Graphic Rendition (SGR) commands interpreted by the terminal or terminal emulator. (See the section in the documentation of your text terminal for permitted values and their meanings as character attributes.) These substring values are integers in decimal representation and can be concatenated with semicolons. grep takes care of assembling the result into a complete SGR sequence ('\33['...'m'). Common values to concatenate include '1' for bold, '4' for underline, '5' for blink, '7' for inverse, '39' for default foreground color, '30' to '37' for foreground colors, '90' to '97' for 16-color mode foreground colors, '38;5;0' to '38;5;255' for 88-color and 256-color modes foreground colors, '49' for default background color, '40' to '47' for background colors, '100' to '107' for 16-color mode background colors, and '48;5;0' to '48;5;255' for 88-color and 256-color modes background colors.

The two-letter names used in the GREP_COLORS environment variable (and some of the others) refer to terminal "capabilities," the ability of a terminal to highlight text, or change its color, and so on. These capabilities are stored in an online database and accessed by the terminfo library.

GREP_OPTIONS

> This variable specifies default options to be placed in front of any explicit options. As this causes problems when writing portable scripts, this feature will be removed in a future release of grep, and grep warns if it is used. Please use an alias or script instead. For example, if grep is in the directory '/usr/bin' you can prepend '$HOME/bin' to your PATH and create an executable script '$HOME/bin/grep' containing the following:

```
#! /bin/sh
export PATH=/usr/bin
exec grep --color=auto --devices=skip "$@"
```

GREP_COLOR

> This variable specifies the color used to highlight matched (non-empty) text. It is deprecated in favor of GREP_COLORS, but still supported. The 'mt', 'ms', and 'mc' capabilities of GREP_COLORS have priority over it. It can only specify the color used to highlight the matching non-empty text in any matching line (a selected line when the '-v' command-line option is omitted, or a context line when '-v' is specified). The default is '01;31', which means a bold red foreground text on the terminal's default background.

`GREP_COLORS`

> This variable specifies the colors and other attributes used to highlight various parts of the output. Its value is a colon-separated list of `terminfo` capabilities that defaults to '`ms=01;31:mc=01;31:sl=:cx=:fn=35:ln=32:bn=32:se=36`' with the '`rv`' and '`ne`' boolean capabilities omitted (i.e., false). Supported capabilities are as follows.

> `sl=`
> > SGR substring for whole selected lines (i.e., matching lines when the '`-v`' command-line option is omitted, or non-matching lines when '`-v`' is specified). If however the boolean '`rv`' capability and the '`-v`' command-line option are both specified, it applies to context matching lines instead. The default is empty (i.e., the terminal's default color pair).

> `cx=`
> > SGR substring for whole context lines (i.e., non-matching lines when the '`-v`' command-line option is omitted, or matching lines when '`-v`' is specified). If however the boolean '`rv`' capability and the '`-v`' command-line option are both specified, it applies to selected non-matching lines instead. The default is empty (i.e., the terminal's default color pair).

> `rv`
> > Boolean value that reverses (swaps) the meanings of the '`sl=`' and '`cx=`' capabilities when the '`-v`' command-line option is specified. The default is false (i.e., the capability is omitted).

> `mt=01;31`
> > SGR substring for matching non-empty text in any matching line (i.e., a selected line when the '`-v`' command-line option is omitted, or a context line when '`-v`' is specified). Setting this is equivalent to setting both '`ms=`' and '`mc=`' at once to the same value. The default is a bold red text foreground over the current line background.

> `ms=01;31`
> > SGR substring for matching non-empty text in a selected line. (This is used only when the '`-v`' command-line option is omitted.) The effect of the '`sl=`' (or '`cx=`' if '`rv`') capability remains active when this takes effect. The default is a bold red text foreground over the current line background.

> `mc=01;31`
> > SGR substring for matching non-empty text in a context line. (This is used only when the '`-v`' command-line option is specified.) The effect of the '`cx=`' (or '`sl=`' if '`rv`') capability remains active when this takes effect. The default is a bold red text foreground over the current line background.

> `fn=35`
> > SGR substring for file names prefixing any content line. The default is a magenta text foreground over the terminal's default background.

> `ln=32`
> > SGR substring for line numbers prefixing any content line. The default is a green text foreground over the terminal's default background.

`bn=32`   SGR substring for byte offsets prefixing any content line. The default is a green text foreground over the terminal's default background.

`se=36`   SGR substring for separators that are inserted between selected line fields ('`:`'), between context line fields ('`-`'), and between groups of adjacent lines when nonzero context is specified ('`--`'). The default is a cyan text foreground over the terminal's default background.

`ne`   Boolean value that prevents clearing to the end of line using Erase in Line (EL) to Right ('`\33[K`') each time a colorized item ends. This is needed on terminals on which EL is not supported. It is otherwise useful on terminals for which the `back_color_erase` (`bce`) boolean `terminfo` capability does not apply, when the chosen highlight colors do not affect the background, or when EL is too slow or causes too much flicker. The default is false (i.e., the capability is omitted).

Note that boolean capabilities have no '`=`'... part. They are omitted (i.e., false) by default and become true when specified.

`LC_ALL`
`LC_COLLATE`
`LANG`   These variables specify the locale for the `LC_COLLATE` category, which might affect how range expressions like '`[a-z]`' are interpreted.

`LC_ALL`
`LC_CTYPE`
`LANG`   These variables specify the locale for the `LC_CTYPE` category, which determines the type of characters, e.g., which characters are whitespace.

`LANGUAGE`
`LC_ALL`
`LC_MESSAGES`
`LANG`   These variables specify the locale for the `LC_MESSAGES` category, which determines the language that `grep` uses for messages. The default '`C`' locale uses American English messages.

`POSIXLY_CORRECT`
       If set, `grep` behaves as POSIX requires; otherwise, `grep` behaves more like other GNU programs. POSIX requires that options that follow file names must be treated as file names; by default, such options are permuted to the front of the operand list and are treated as options. Also, `POSIXLY_CORRECT` disables special handling of an invalid bracket expression. See [invalid-bracket-expr], page 15.

`_N_GNU_nonoption_argv_flags_`
       (Here *N* is `grep`'s numeric process ID.) If the *i*th character of this environment variable's value is '`1`', do not consider the *i*th operand of `grep` to be an option, even if it appears to be one. A shell can put this variable in the environment for each command it runs, specifying which operands are the results of file name wildcard expansion and therefore should not be treated as options. This

behavior is available only with the GNU C library, and only when `POSIXLY_` `CORRECT` is not set.

2.3 Exit Status

Normally the exit status is 0 if a line is selected, 1 if no lines were selected, and 2 if an error occurred. However, if the '`-q`' or '`--quiet`' or '`--silent`' option is used and a line is selected, the exit status is 0 even if an error occurred. Other `grep` implementations may exit with status greater than 2 on error.

2.4 grep Programs

`grep` searches the named input files for lines containing a match to the given pattern. By default, `grep` prints the matching lines. A file named '`-`' stands for standard input. If no input is specified, `grep` searches the working directory '`.`' if given a command-line option specifying recursion; otherwise, `grep` searches standard input. There are four major variants of `grep`, controlled by the following options.

'`-G`'
'`--basic-regexp`'
> Interpret the pattern as a basic regular expression (BRE). This is the default.

'`-E`'
'`--extended-regexp`'
> Interpret the pattern as an extended regular expression (ERE). ('`-E`' is specified by POSIX.)

'`-F`'
'`--fixed-strings`'
> Interpret the pattern as a list of fixed strings, separated by newlines, any of which is to be matched. ('`-F`' is specified by POSIX.)

'`-P`'
'`--perl-regexp`'
> Interpret the pattern as a Perl regular expression. This is highly experimental and '`grep -P`' may warn of unimplemented features.

In addition, two variant programs `egrep` and `fgrep` are available. `egrep` is the same as '`grep -E`'. `fgrep` is the same as '`grep -F`'. Direct invocation as either `egrep` or `fgrep` is deprecated, but is provided to allow historical applications that rely on them to run unmodified.

3 Regular Expressions

A *regular expression* is a pattern that describes a set of strings. Regular expressions are constructed analogously to arithmetic expressions, by using various operators to combine smaller expressions. `grep` understands three different versions of regular expression syntax: "basic," (BRE) "extended" (ERE) and "perl". In GNU `grep`, there is no difference in available functionality between the basic and extended syntaxes. In other implementations, basic regular expressions are less powerful. The following description applies to extended regular expressions; differences for basic regular expressions are summarized afterwards. Perl regular expressions give additional functionality, and are documented in the *pcresyntax*(3) and *pcrepattern*(3) manual pages, but may not be available on every system.

3.1 Fundamental Structure

The fundamental building blocks are the regular expressions that match a single character. Most characters, including all letters and digits, are regular expressions that match themselves. Any meta-character with special meaning may be quoted by preceding it with a backslash.

A regular expression may be followed by one of several repetition operators:

'.'   The period '.' matches any single character.

'?'   The preceding item is optional and will be matched at most once.

'*'   The preceding item will be matched zero or more times.

'+'   The preceding item will be matched one or more times.

'{n}'   The preceding item is matched exactly *n* times.

'{n,}'   The preceding item is matched *n* or more times.

'{,m}'   The preceding item is matched at most *m* times. This is a GNU extension.

'{n,m}'   The preceding item is matched at least *n* times, but not more than *m* times.

The empty regular expression matches the empty string. Two regular expressions may be concatenated; the resulting regular expression matches any string formed by concatenating two substrings that respectively match the concatenated expressions.

Two regular expressions may be joined by the infix operator '|'; the resulting regular expression matches any string matching either alternate expression.

Repetition takes precedence over concatenation, which in turn takes precedence over alternation. A whole expression may be enclosed in parentheses to override these precedence rules and form a subexpression. An unmatched ')' matches just itself.

3.2 Character Classes and Bracket Expressions

A *bracket expression* is a list of characters enclosed by '[' and ']'. It matches any single character in that list; if the first character of the list is the caret '^', then it matches any character **not** in the list. For example, the regular expression '[0123456789]' matches any single digit.

Within a bracket expression, a *range expression* consists of two characters separated by a hyphen. It matches any single character that sorts between the two characters, inclusive. In the default C locale, the sorting sequence is the native character order; for example, '[a-d]' is equivalent to '[abcd]'. In other locales, the sorting sequence is not specified, and '[a-d]' might be equivalent to '[abcd]' or to '[aBbCcDd]', or it might fail to match any character, or the set of characters that it matches might even be erratic. To obtain the traditional interpretation of bracket expressions, you can use the 'C' locale by setting the LC_ALL environment variable to the value 'C'.

Finally, certain named classes of characters are predefined within bracket expressions, as follows. Their interpretation depends on the LC_CTYPE locale; for example, '[[:alnum:]]' means the character class of numbers and letters in the current locale.

'[:alnum:]'

> Alphanumeric characters: '[:alpha:]' and '[:digit:]'; in the 'C' locale and ASCII character encoding, this is the same as '[0-9A-Za-z]'.

'[:alpha:]'

> Alphabetic characters: '[:lower:]' and '[:upper:]'; in the 'C' locale and ASCII character encoding, this is the same as '[A-Za-z]'.

'[:blank:]'

> Blank characters: space and tab.

'[:cntrl:]'

> Control characters. In ASCII, these characters have octal codes 000 through 037, and 177 (DEL). In other character sets, these are the equivalent characters, if any.

'[:digit:]'

> Digits: 0 1 2 3 4 5 6 7 8 9.

'[:graph:]'

> Graphical characters: '[:alnum:]' and '[:punct:]'.

'[:lower:]'

> Lower-case letters; in the 'C' locale and ASCII character encoding, this is a b c d e f g h i j k l m n o p q r s t u v w x y z.

'[:print:]'

> Printable characters: '[:alnum:]', '[:punct:]', and space.

'[:punct:]'

> Punctuation characters; in the 'C' locale and ASCII character encoding, this is ! " # $ % & ' ( ) * + , - . / : ; < = > ? @ [\ ] ^ _ ` { | } ~.

'[:space:]'

> Space characters: in the 'C' locale, this is tab, newline, vertical tab, form feed, carriage return, and space. See Chapter 4 [Usage], page 17, for more discussion of matching newlines.

'[:upper:]'

> Upper-case letters: in the 'C' locale and ASCII character encoding, this is A B C D E F G H I J K L M N O P Q R S T U V W X Y Z.

'[:xdigit:]'

> Hexadecimal digits: 0 1 2 3 4 5 6 7 8 9 A B C D E F a b c d e f.

Note that the brackets in these class names are part of the symbolic names, and must be included in addition to the brackets delimiting the bracket expression.

If you mistakenly omit the outer brackets, and search for say, '[:upper:]', GNU grep prints a diagnostic and exits with status 2, on the assumption that you did not intend to search for the nominally equivalent regular expression: '[:epru]'. Set the POSIXLY_CORRECT environment variable to disable this feature.

Most meta-characters lose their special meaning inside bracket expressions.

']'   ends the bracket expression if it's not the first list item. So, if you want to make the ']' character a list item, you must put it first.

'[.'   represents the open collating symbol.

'.]'   represents the close collating symbol.

'[='   represents the open equivalence class.

'=]'   represents the close equivalence class.

'[:'   represents the open character class symbol, and should be followed by a valid character class name.

':]'   represents the close character class symbol.

'-'   represents the range if it's not first or last in a list or the ending point of a range.

'^'   represents the characters not in the list. If you want to make the '^' character a list item, place it anywhere but first.

3.3 The Backslash Character and Special Expressions

The '\' character, when followed by certain ordinary characters, takes a special meaning:

'\b'   Match the empty string at the edge of a word.

'\B'   Match the empty string provided it's not at the edge of a word.

'\<'   Match the empty string at the beginning of word.

'\>'   Match the empty string at the end of word.

'\w'   Match word constituent, it is a synonym for '[_[:alnum:]]'.

'\W'   Match non-word constituent, it is a synonym for '[^_[:alnum:]]'.

'\s'   Match whitespace, it is a synonym for '[[:space:]]'.

'\S'   Match non-whitespace, it is a synonym for '[^[:space:]]'.

For example, '\brat\b' matches the separate word 'rat', '\Brat\B' matches 'crate' but not 'furry rat'.

3.4 Anchoring

The caret '^' and the dollar sign '$' are meta-characters that respectively match the empty string at the beginning and end of a line. They are termed *anchors*, since they force the match to be "anchored" to beginning or end of a line, respectively.

3.5 Back-references and Subexpressions

The back-reference '\n', where n is a single digit, matches the substring previously matched by the nth parenthesized subexpression of the regular expression. For example, '(a)\1' matches 'aa'. When used with alternation, if the group does not participate in the match then the back-reference makes the whole match fail. For example, 'a(.)|b\1' will not match 'ba'. When multiple regular expressions are given with '-e' or from a file ('-f *file*'), back-references are local to each expression.

3.6 Basic vs Extended Regular Expressions

In basic regular expressions the meta-characters '?', '+', '{', '|', '(', and ')' lose their special meaning; instead use the backslashed versions '\?', '\+', '\{', '\|', '\(', and '\)'.

Traditional **egrep** did not support the '{' meta-character, and some **egrep** implementations support '\{' instead, so portable scripts should avoid '{' in 'grep -E' patterns and should use '[{]' to match a literal '{'.

GNU **grep** -E attempts to support traditional usage by assuming that '{' is not special if it would be the start of an invalid interval specification. For example, the command 'grep -E '{1'' searches for the two-character string '{1' instead of reporting a syntax error in the regular expression. POSIX allows this behavior as an extension, but portable scripts should avoid it.

4 Usage

Here is an example command that invokes GNU grep:

```
grep -i 'hello.*world' menu.h main.c
```

This lists all lines in the files 'menu.h' and 'main.c' that contain the string 'hello' followed by the string 'world'; this is because '.*' matches zero or more characters within a line. See Chapter 3 [Regular Expressions], page 13. The '-i' option causes grep to ignore case, causing it to match the line 'Hello, world!', which it would not otherwise match. See Chapter 2 [Invoking], page 2, for more details about how to invoke grep.

Here are some common questions and answers about grep usage.

1. How can I list just the names of matching files?

    ```
    grep -l 'main' *.c
    ```

    lists the names of all C files in the current directory whose contents mention 'main'.

2. How do I search directories recursively?

    ```
    grep -r 'hello' /home/gigi
    ```

    searches for 'hello' in all files under the '/home/gigi' directory. For more control over which files are searched, use find, grep, and xargs. For example, the following command searches only C files:

    ```
    find /home/gigi -name '*.c' -print0 | xargs -0r grep -H 'hello'
    ```

    This differs from the command:

    ```
    grep -H 'hello' *.c
    ```

    which merely looks for 'hello' in all files in the current directory whose names end in '.c'. The 'find ...' command line above is more similar to the command:

    ```
    grep -rH --include='*.c' 'hello' /home/gigi
    ```

3. What if a pattern has a leading '-'?

    ```
    grep -e '--cut here--' *
    ```

    searches for all lines matching '--cut here--'. Without '-e', grep would attempt to parse '--cut here--' as a list of options.

4. Suppose I want to search for a whole word, not a part of a word?

    ```
    grep -w 'hello' *
    ```

    searches only for instances of 'hello' that are entire words; it does not match 'Othello'. For more control, use '\<' and '\>' to match the start and end of words. For example:

    ```
    grep 'hello\>' *
    ```

    searches only for words ending in 'hello', so it matches the word 'Othello'.

5. How do I output context around the matching lines?

    ```
    grep -C 2 'hello' *
    ```

    prints two lines of context around each matching line.

6. How do I force grep to print the name of the file?

    Append '/dev/null':

    ```
    grep 'eli' /etc/passwd /dev/null
    ```

    gets you:

```
/etc/passwd:eli:x:2098:1000:Eli Smith:/home/eli:/bin/bash
```
Alternatively, use '-H', which is a GNU extension:

```
grep -H 'eli' /etc/passwd
```

7. Why do people use strange regular expressions on `ps` output?

```
ps -ef | grep '[c]ron'
```

If the pattern had been written without the square brackets, it would have matched not only the `ps` output line for `cron`, but also the `ps` output line for `grep`. Note that on some platforms, `ps` limits the output to the width of the screen; `grep` does not have any limit on the length of a line except the available memory.

8. Why does `grep` report "Binary file matches"?

If `grep` listed all matching "lines" from a binary file, it would probably generate output that is not useful, and it might even muck up your display. So GNU `grep` suppresses output from files that appear to be binary files. To force GNU `grep` to output lines even from files that appear to be binary, use the '-a' or '--binary-files=text' option. To eliminate the "Binary file matches" messages, use the '-I' or '--binary-files=without-match' option.

9. Why doesn't 'grep -lv' print non-matching file names?

'grep -lv' lists the names of all files containing one or more lines that do not match. To list the names of all files that contain no matching lines, use the '-L' or '--files-without-match' option.

10. I can do "OR" with '|', but what about "AND"?

```
grep 'paul' /etc/motd | grep 'franc,ois'
```

finds all lines that contain both 'paul' and 'franc,ois'.

11. Why does the empty pattern match every input line?

The `grep` command searches for lines that contain strings that match a pattern. Every line contains the empty string, so an empty pattern causes `grep` to find a match on each line. It is not the only such pattern: '^', '$', '.*', and many other patterns cause `grep` to match every line.

To match empty lines, use the pattern '^$'. To match blank lines, use the pattern '^[[:blank:]]*$'. To match no lines at all, use the command 'grep -f /dev/null'.

12. How can I search in both standard input and in files?

Use the special file name '-':

```
cat /etc/passwd | grep 'alain' - /etc/motd
```

13. How to express palindromes in a regular expression?

It can be done by using back-references; for example, a palindrome of 4 characters can be written with a BRE:

```
grep -w -e '\(.\)\(.\).\2\1' file
```

It matches the word "radar" or "civic."

Guglielmo Bondioni proposed a single RE that finds all palindromes up to 19 characters long using 9 subexpressions and 9 back-references:

```
grep -E -e '^(.?)(.?)(.?)(.?)(.?)(.?)(.?)(.?)(.?).?\9\8\7\6\5\4\3\2\1$' file
```

Note this is done by using GNU ERE extensions; it might not be portable to other implementations of `grep`.

14. Why is this back-reference failing?

```
echo 'ba' | grep -E '(a)\1|b\1'
```

This gives no output, because the first alternate '(a)\1' does not match, as there is no 'aa' in the input, so the '\1' in the second alternate has nothing to refer back to, meaning it will never match anything. (The second alternate in this example can only match if the first alternate has matched—making the second one superfluous.)

15. How can I match across lines?

Standard grep cannot do this, as it is fundamentally line-based. Therefore, merely using the [:space:] character class does not match newlines in the way you might expect.

With the GNU grep option '-z' ('--null-data'), each input "line" is terminated by a null byte; see Section 2.1.7 [Other Options], page 8. Thus, you can match newlines in the input, but typically if there is a match the entire input is output, so this usage is often combined with output-suppressing options like '-q', e.g.:

```
printf 'foo\nbar\n' | grep -z -q 'foo[[:space:]]\+bar'
```

If this does not suffice, you can transform the input before giving it to grep, or turn to awk, sed, perl, or many other utilities that are designed to operate across lines.

16. What do grep, fgrep, and egrep stand for?

The name grep comes from the way line editing was done on Unix. For example, ed uses the following syntax to print a list of matching lines on the screen:

```
global/regular expression/print
g/re/p
```

fgrep stands for Fixed grep; egrep stands for Extended grep.

5 Reporting bugs

Bug reports can be found at the GNU bug report logs for `grep`. If you find a bug not listed there, please email it to `bug-grep@gnu.org` to create a new bug report.

5.1 Known Bugs

Large repetition counts in the '`{n,m}`' construct may cause `grep` to use lots of memory. In addition, certain other obscure regular expressions require exponential time and space, and may cause `grep` to run out of memory.

Back-references are very slow, and may require exponential time.

6 Copying

GNU `grep` is licensed under the GNU GPL, which makes it *free software*.

The "free" in "free software" refers to liberty, not price. As some GNU project advocates like to point out, think of "free speech" rather than "free beer". In short, you have the right (freedom) to run and change `grep` and distribute it to other people, and—if you want—charge money for doing either. The important restriction is that you have to grant your recipients the same rights and impose the same restrictions.

This general method of licensing software is sometimes called *open source*. The GNU project prefers the term "free software" for reasons outlined at `http://www.gnu.org/philosophy/open-source-misses-the-point.html`.

This manual is free documentation in the same sense. The documentation license is included below. The license for the program is available with the source code, or at `http://www.gnu.org/licenses/gpl.html`.

6.1 GNU Free Documentation License

Version 1.3, 3 November 2008

Copyright © 2000, 2001, 2002, 2007, 2008 Free Software Foundation, Inc.
`http://fsf.org/`

Everyone is permitted to copy and distribute verbatim copies
of this license document, but changing it is not allowed.

0. PREAMBLE

The purpose of this License is to make a manual, textbook, or other functional and useful document *free* in the sense of freedom: to assure everyone the effective freedom to copy and redistribute it, with or without modifying it, either commercially or non-commercially. Secondarily, this License preserves for the author and publisher a way to get credit for their work, while not being considered responsible for modifications made by others.

This License is a kind of "copyleft", which means that derivative works of the document must themselves be free in the same sense. It complements the GNU General Public License, which is a copyleft license designed for free software.

We have designed this License in order to use it for manuals for free software, because free software needs free documentation: a free program should come with manuals providing the same freedoms that the software does. But this License is not limited to software manuals; it can be used for any textual work, regardless of subject matter or whether it is published as a printed book. We recommend this License principally for works whose purpose is instruction or reference.

1. APPLICABILITY AND DEFINITIONS

This License applies to any manual or other work, in any medium, that contains a notice placed by the copyright holder saying it can be distributed under the terms of this License. Such a notice grants a world-wide, royalty-free license, unlimited in duration, to use that work under the conditions stated herein. The "Document", below, refers to any such manual or work. Any member of the public is a licensee, and is addressed as "you". You accept the license if you copy, modify or distribute the work in a way requiring permission under copyright law.

A "Modified Version" of the Document means any work containing the Document or a portion of it, either copied verbatim, or with modifications and/or translated into another language.

A "Secondary Section" is a named appendix or a front-matter section of the Document that deals exclusively with the relationship of the publishers or authors of the Document to the Document's overall subject (or to related matters) and contains nothing that could fall directly within that overall subject. (Thus, if the Document is in part a textbook of mathematics, a Secondary Section may not explain any mathematics.) The relationship could be a matter of historical connection with the subject or with related matters, or of legal, commercial, philosophical, ethical or political position regarding them.

The "Invariant Sections" are certain Secondary Sections whose titles are designated, as being those of Invariant Sections, in the notice that says that the Document is released under this License. If a section does not fit the above definition of Secondary then it is not allowed to be designated as Invariant. The Document may contain zero Invariant Sections. If the Document does not identify any Invariant Sections then there are none.

The "Cover Texts" are certain short passages of text that are listed, as Front-Cover Texts or Back-Cover Texts, in the notice that says that the Document is released under this License. A Front-Cover Text may be at most 5 words, and a Back-Cover Text may be at most 25 words.

A "Transparent" copy of the Document means a machine-readable copy, represented in a format whose specification is available to the general public, that is suitable for revising the document straightforwardly with generic text editors or (for images composed of pixels) generic paint programs or (for drawings) some widely available drawing editor, and that is suitable for input to text formatters or for automatic translation to a variety of formats suitable for input to text formatters. A copy made in an otherwise Transparent file format whose markup, or absence of markup, has been arranged to thwart or discourage subsequent modification by readers is not Transparent. An image format is not Transparent if used for any substantial amount of text. A copy that is not "Transparent" is called "Opaque".

Examples of suitable formats for Transparent copies include plain ASCII without markup, Texinfo input format, LaTeX input format, SGML or XML using a publicly available DTD, and standard-conforming simple HTML, PostScript or PDF designed for human modification. Examples of transparent image formats include PNG, XCF and JPG. Opaque formats include proprietary formats that can be read and edited only by proprietary word processors, SGML or XML for which the DTD and/or processing tools are not generally available, and the machine-generated HTML, PostScript or PDF produced by some word processors for output purposes only.

The "Title Page" means, for a printed book, the title page itself, plus such following pages as are needed to hold, legibly, the material this License requires to appear in the title page. For works in formats which do not have any title page as such, "Title Page" means the text near the most prominent appearance of the work's title, preceding the beginning of the body of the text.

The "publisher" means any person or entity that distributes copies of the Document to the public.

A section "Entitled XYZ" means a named subunit of the Document whose title either is precisely XYZ or contains XYZ in parentheses following text that translates XYZ in another language. (Here XYZ stands for a specific section name mentioned below, such as "Acknowledgements", "Dedications", "Endorsements", or "History".) To "Preserve the Title" of such a section when you modify the Document means that it remains a section "Entitled XYZ" according to this definition.

The Document may include Warranty Disclaimers next to the notice which states that this License applies to the Document. These Warranty Disclaimers are considered to be included by reference in this License, but only as regards disclaiming warranties: any other implication that these Warranty Disclaimers may have is void and has no effect on the meaning of this License.

2. VERBATIM COPYING

You may copy and distribute the Document in any medium, either commercially or noncommercially, provided that this License, the copyright notices, and the license notice saying this License applies to the Document are reproduced in all copies, and that you add no other conditions whatsoever to those of this License. You may not use technical measures to obstruct or control the reading or further copying of the copies you make or distribute. However, you may accept compensation in exchange for copies. If you distribute a large enough number of copies you must also follow the conditions in section 3.

You may also lend copies, under the same conditions stated above, and you may publicly display copies.

3. COPYING IN QUANTITY

If you publish printed copies (or copies in media that commonly have printed covers) of the Document, numbering more than 100, and the Document's license notice requires Cover Texts, you must enclose the copies in covers that carry, clearly and legibly, all these Cover Texts: Front-Cover Texts on the front cover, and Back-Cover Texts on the back cover. Both covers must also clearly and legibly identify you as the publisher of these copies. The front cover must present the full title with all words of the title equally prominent and visible. You may add other material on the covers in addition. Copying with changes limited to the covers, as long as they preserve the title of the Document and satisfy these conditions, can be treated as verbatim copying in other respects.

If the required texts for either cover are too voluminous to fit legibly, you should put the first ones listed (as many as fit reasonably) on the actual cover, and continue the rest onto adjacent pages.

If you publish or distribute Opaque copies of the Document numbering more than 100, you must either include a machine-readable Transparent copy along with each Opaque copy, or state in or with each Opaque copy a computer-network location from which the general network-using public has access to download using public-standard network protocols a complete Transparent copy of the Document, free of added material. If you use the latter option, you must take reasonably prudent steps, when you begin distribution of Opaque copies in quantity, to ensure that this Transparent copy will remain thus accessible at the stated location until at least one year after the last time you distribute an Opaque copy (directly or through your agents or retailers) of that edition to the public.

It is requested, but not required, that you contact the authors of the Document well before redistributing any large number of copies, to give them a chance to provide you with an updated version of the Document.

4. MODIFICATIONS

You may copy and distribute a Modified Version of the Document under the conditions of sections 2 and 3 above, provided that you release the Modified Version under precisely this License, with the Modified Version filling the role of the Document, thus licensing distribution and modification of the Modified Version to whoever possesses a copy of it. In addition, you must do these things in the Modified Version:

A. Use in the Title Page (and on the covers, if any) a title distinct from that of the Document, and from those of previous versions (which should, if there were any, be listed in the History section of the Document). You may use the same title as a previous version if the original publisher of that version gives permission.

B. List on the Title Page, as authors, one or more persons or entities responsible for authorship of the modifications in the Modified Version, together with at least five of the principal authors of the Document (all of its principal authors, if it has fewer than five), unless they release you from this requirement.

C. State on the Title page the name of the publisher of the Modified Version, as the publisher.

D. Preserve all the copyright notices of the Document.

E. Add an appropriate copyright notice for your modifications adjacent to the other copyright notices.

F. Include, immediately after the copyright notices, a license notice giving the public permission to use the Modified Version under the terms of this License, in the form shown in the Addendum below.

G. Preserve in that license notice the full lists of Invariant Sections and required Cover Texts given in the Document's license notice.

H. Include an unaltered copy of this License.

I. Preserve the section Entitled "History", Preserve its Title, and add to it an item stating at least the title, year, new authors, and publisher of the Modified Version as given on the Title Page. If there is no section Entitled "History" in the Document, create one stating the title, year, authors, and publisher of the Document as given on its Title Page, then add an item describing the Modified Version as stated in the previous sentence.

J. Preserve the network location, if any, given in the Document for public access to a Transparent copy of the Document, and likewise the network locations given in the Document for previous versions it was based on. These may be placed in the "History" section. You may omit a network location for a work that was published at least four years before the Document itself, or if the original publisher of the version it refers to gives permission.

K. For any section Entitled "Acknowledgements" or "Dedications", Preserve the Title of the section, and preserve in the section all the substance and tone of each of the contributor acknowledgements and/or dedications given therein.

L. Preserve all the Invariant Sections of the Document, unaltered in their text and in their titles. Section numbers or the equivalent are not considered part of the section titles.

M. Delete any section Entitled "Endorsements". Such a section may not be included in the Modified Version.

N. Do not retitle any existing section to be Entitled "Endorsements" or to conflict in title with any Invariant Section.

O. Preserve any Warranty Disclaimers.

If the Modified Version includes new front-matter sections or appendices that qualify as Secondary Sections and contain no material copied from the Document, you may at your option designate some or all of these sections as invariant. To do this, add their titles to the list of Invariant Sections in the Modified Version's license notice. These titles must be distinct from any other section titles.

You may add a section Entitled "Endorsements", provided it contains nothing but endorsements of your Modified Version by various parties—for example, statements of peer review or that the text has been approved by an organization as the authoritative definition of a standard.

You may add a passage of up to five words as a Front-Cover Text, and a passage of up to 25 words as a Back-Cover Text, to the end of the list of Cover Texts in the Modified Version. Only one passage of Front-Cover Text and one of Back-Cover Text may be added by (or through arrangements made by) any one entity. If the Document already includes a cover text for the same cover, previously added by you or by arrangement made by the same entity you are acting on behalf of, you may not add another; but you may replace the old one, on explicit permission from the previous publisher that added the old one.

The author(s) and publisher(s) of the Document do not by this License give permission to use their names for publicity for or to assert or imply endorsement of any Modified Version.

5. COMBINING DOCUMENTS

You may combine the Document with other documents released under this License, under the terms defined in section 4 above for modified versions, provided that you include in the combination all of the Invariant Sections of all of the original documents, unmodified, and list them all as Invariant Sections of your combined work in its license notice, and that you preserve all their Warranty Disclaimers.

The combined work need only contain one copy of this License, and multiple identical Invariant Sections may be replaced with a single copy. If there are multiple Invariant Sections with the same name but different contents, make the title of each such section unique by adding at the end of it, in parentheses, the name of the original author or publisher of that section if known, or else a unique number. Make the same adjustment to the section titles in the list of Invariant Sections in the license notice of the combined work.

In the combination, you must combine any sections Entitled "History" in the various original documents, forming one section Entitled "History"; likewise combine any sections Entitled "Acknowledgements", and any sections Entitled "Dedications". You must delete all sections Entitled "Endorsements."

6. COLLECTIONS OF DOCUMENTS

You may make a collection consisting of the Document and other documents released under this License, and replace the individual copies of this License in the various documents with a single copy that is included in the collection, provided that you follow the rules of this License for verbatim copying of each of the documents in all other respects.

You may extract a single document from such a collection, and distribute it individually under this License, provided you insert a copy of this License into the extracted document, and follow this License in all other respects regarding verbatim copying of that document.

7. AGGREGATION WITH INDEPENDENT WORKS

A compilation of the Document or its derivatives with other separate and independent documents or works, in or on a volume of a storage or distribution medium, is called an "aggregate" if the copyright resulting from the compilation is not used to limit the legal rights of the compilation's users beyond what the individual works permit. When the Document is included in an aggregate, this License does not apply to the other works in the aggregate which are not themselves derivative works of the Document.

If the Cover Text requirement of section 3 is applicable to these copies of the Document, then if the Document is less than one half of the entire aggregate, the Document's Cover Texts may be placed on covers that bracket the Document within the aggregate, or the electronic equivalent of covers if the Document is in electronic form. Otherwise they must appear on printed covers that bracket the whole aggregate.

8. TRANSLATION

Translation is considered a kind of modification, so you may distribute translations of the Document under the terms of section 4. Replacing Invariant Sections with translations requires special permission from their copyright holders, but you may include translations of some or all Invariant Sections in addition to the original versions of these Invariant Sections. You may include a translation of this License, and all the license notices in the Document, and any Warranty Disclaimers, provided that you also include the original English version of this License and the original versions of those notices and disclaimers. In case of a disagreement between the translation and the original version of this License or a notice or disclaimer, the original version will prevail.

If a section in the Document is Entitled "Acknowledgements", "Dedications", or "History", the requirement (section 4) to Preserve its Title (section 1) will typically require changing the actual title.

9. TERMINATION

You may not copy, modify, sublicense, or distribute the Document except as expressly provided under this License. Any attempt otherwise to copy, modify, sublicense, or distribute it is void, and will automatically terminate your rights under this License.

However, if you cease all violation of this License, then your license from a particular copyright holder is reinstated (a) provisionally, unless and until the copyright holder explicitly and finally terminates your license, and (b) permanently, if the copyright holder fails to notify you of the violation by some reasonable means prior to 60 days after the cessation.

Moreover, your license from a particular copyright holder is reinstated permanently if the copyright holder notifies you of the violation by some reasonable means, this is the first time you have received notice of violation of this License (for any work) from that copyright holder, and you cure the violation prior to 30 days after your receipt of the notice.

Termination of your rights under this section does not terminate the licenses of parties who have received copies or rights from you under this License. If your rights have been terminated and not permanently reinstated, receipt of a copy of some or all of the same material does not give you any rights to use it.

10. FUTURE REVISIONS OF THIS LICENSE

The Free Software Foundation may publish new, revised versions of the GNU Free Documentation License from time to time. Such new versions will be similar in spirit to the present version, but may differ in detail to address new problems or concerns. See http://www.gnu.org/copyleft/.

Each version of the License is given a distinguishing version number. If the Document specifies that a particular numbered version of this License "or any later version" applies to it, you have the option of following the terms and conditions either of that specified version or of any later version that has been published (not as a draft) by the Free Software Foundation. If the Document does not specify a version number of this License, you may choose any version ever published (not as a draft) by the Free Software Foundation. If the Document specifies that a proxy can decide which future versions of this License can be used, that proxy's public statement of acceptance of a version permanently authorizes you to choose that version for the Document.

11. RELICENSING

"Massive Multiauthor Collaboration Site" (or "MMC Site") means any World Wide Web server that publishes copyrightable works and also provides prominent facilities for anybody to edit those works. A public wiki that anybody can edit is an example of such a server. A "Massive Multiauthor Collaboration" (or "MMC") contained in the site means any set of copyrightable works thus published on the MMC site.

"CC-BY-SA" means the Creative Commons Attribution-Share Alike 3.0 license published by Creative Commons Corporation, a not-for-profit corporation with a principal place of business in San Francisco, California, as well as future copyleft versions of that license published by that same organization.

"Incorporate" means to publish or republish a Document, in whole or in part, as part of another Document.

An MMC is "eligible for relicensing" if it is licensed under this License, and if all works that were first published under this License somewhere other than this MMC, and subsequently incorporated in whole or in part into the MMC, (1) had no cover texts or invariant sections, and (2) were thus incorporated prior to November 1, 2008.

The operator of an MMC Site may republish an MMC contained in the site under CC-BY-SA on the same site at any time before August 1, 2009, provided the MMC is eligible for relicensing.

ADDENDUM: How to use this License for your documents

To use this License in a document you have written, include a copy of the License in the document and put the following copyright and license notices just after the title page:

```
Copyright (C)  year  your name.
Permission is granted to copy, distribute and/or modify this document
under the terms of the GNU Free Documentation License, Version 1.3
or any later version published by the Free Software Foundation;
with no Invariant Sections, no Front-Cover Texts, and no Back-Cover
Texts.  A copy of the license is included in the section entitled ''GNU
Free Documentation License''.
```

If you have Invariant Sections, Front-Cover Texts and Back-Cover Texts, replace the "with...Texts." line with this:

```
with the Invariant Sections being list their titles, with
the Front-Cover Texts being list, and with the Back-Cover Texts
being list.
```

If you have Invariant Sections without Cover Texts, or some other combination of the three, merge those two alternatives to suit the situation.

If your document contains nontrivial examples of program code, we recommend releasing these examples in parallel under your choice of free software license, such as the GNU General Public License, to permit their use in free software.

Index